Grow [Up in My] Little Italy

A POETIC MEMOIR OF NORTHSIDE ENDICOTT IN THE 30's & 40's

Dominick Tammetta, Ph.D

© 2009 Domenico Press, Deposit, New York.

Published by
DatASIA, Inc., Holmes Beach, Florida 34218.
All rights reserved.

Production Credits
Typesetting: Margaret Tammetta
Book layout and design: Kristen Tuttle

ISBN: 978-1-934431-99-3
Library of Congress Pre-Assigned Control Number: 2009926685
Printed in the United States of America.
First Edition.

Dedication

To my wife and my children
I leave my love, my words and
my memories.

Acknowledgements
❧☙

*T*he ideas for writing this first collection of poetry followed the writing of my memoir which took my life up to the year 2000. In perusing that material, I saw nostalgic slices of memory which lent themselves to a poetic format and thus, a book idea took hold.

I am grateful to many who helped in its fruition: To Fran Battisti and Angelo Zuccolo for their early support. To Paul Van Savage for his search for photos and persistent interest. To Loretta Swit, a lifelong friend of my wife's for her endorsement. To Anthony Vetrano for his invaluable writing suggestions and his endorsement. And to Gene Iannone who contributed with old photographs, along with historical information as he rekindled my memory with his encyclopedic knowledge of the Nob.

There are many others who contributed with ideas and photos: Fulton Lewis with his computer expertise, Joshua and Jonah Tammetta for the use of their photos on the cover. Others include: Joe Randesi, Jim Antonelli, Tony Iacovelli, John Meany, Julie Savich-Hardy, Scott and Peter Tammetta, Fernanda Rotunno, Angie Wallace, Terry Cribbs and Peter Antonsen. The poetry anthology "Unsettling America" edited by Maria Mazziotti Gillan and Jennifer Gillan, helped in my further understanding of the immigrant experience. I am indebted to Kristen Tuttle, our graphic designer, a talented and artistic professional who was always approachable and patient with first time self publishers.

And lastly, I am grateful to my wife who handled the considerable typesetting of this entire project. She unraveled some of the confusion we experienced with the computer; she endured my persistent pleas for assistance and she offered many insightful ideas.

Table of Contents

Introduction

As a first generation Italian-American who was raised and schooled on the Northside of Endicott, N.Y., it has nearly been 50 years since I left that upbringing and its memories. Returning for visits there throughout the years, it has become clear that its face has changed considerably. Browsing around the neighborhoods that I had intimately known, the changes from the perspective of one who has been away seem especially obvious. The characteristic sounds are missing: the pervasive spoken Italian and nostalgic Old World music. What was the old St. Anthony's church is now a corporate office. Our old elementary school houses a Protestant church center. Various transient groups with cultural roots different from our previous ethnic culture have replaced many of the formerly dominant Italian households.

In recent years, the economy has slackened with a widespread loss of jobs resulting in a lower standard of living and a poorer quality of life for its residents. Gone are most of the mom and pop grocery stores which in the past were filled to the ceiling with imported Italian specialities, as customers were surrounded by open barrels of olives and beans and a variety of cheeses hanging from hooks. Gone are the spiedie stands fronting small bars attended by old men in white aprons which lent the area a quaint Old World charm. Holiday fests which were typically fun-filled with ethnic delicacies and music, today appear more raucous and more like rock concerts. Clearly, life is different on the Hill today. Much of the above is a product of natural attrition. Walk down any Main Street in most American cities and the changes are similar. What is unusual, however, is the irrevocable loss of an earlier culture bred out of the large immigrant population that settled in communities like Endicott in the early part of the 20th century. The lifestyles of these settlers were blends of the Old and New Worlds, resulting in an unusual hybrid culture whose memory begs to be preserved. The Little Italy project is dedicated to preserve this once predominant Italian-American culture through its encouragement of Italian-friendly businesses and its sponsorship of tasteful and artistic cultural events.

This collection of poems presents a modest attempt to complement this effort. They are storied recollections told through poems that describe in part what life was like on the Northside growing up in the 30's and 40's in its schools, its churches, and a community in general. Consider them as a series of snapshots arbitrarily chosen to reflect significant but limited aspects of community life on Endicott's Northside.
They are a potpourri of memories and personal reflections which past residents may identify and probably embellish.

My father was born in Fondi, Province of Latina, Italy in 1902. It is located between Rome and Naples in the Compania district. He emigrated to this country in 1919 and began work with the Endicott-Johnson Corporation where he was employed for the rest of his life. He married my mother in 1926. It may be noticeable that reference to my mother, Aurora, are lacking in this writing. She was a Mexican immigrant who became immersed in my father's native heritage, and like so many immigrant families, traditionally accepted his dominant role as the male head of the household. Through the years my mother was able to understand spoken Italian and mingled well with her neighbors who, like her spouse, had left Italy for the American dream and a better life.

While history if rife with its accounts of rejection, oppression and discrimination of immigrants making their way into the American mainstream, the sociology of this story is somewhat different and has more positive outcomes. The large waves of Europeans emigrated to this country in the first quarter of the 20th century and they began the long and difficult process of assimilation and acculturation to preserve their respective languages and cultural values. So, too, did the Italians who established their community in Endicott. They became largely employed by a paternalistic employer, the Endicott-Johnson Shoe Corporation, which provided for them and their families an array of generous benefits – medical, dental, recreational and even housing to enhance their interest and affiliations. Most of these immigrants settled in a particular part of the Village, somewhat geographically removed from the mainstream, on a hill, with the Erie railroad tracks serving as a dividing line between the North and South sides. Here they shared their lives together at work and in their neighborhoods, literally rubbing shoulders on a daily basis. They did not need to alter their values or their ways as did other minority groups in their attempts to become assimilated. There was strength in numbers. They defined themselves. This is not to deny the successes of other ethnic groups on the Hill. Rather, the focus here is on a particular group with which this writer can identify.

Undoubtedly, there were numerous instances of discrimination and crime which another narrative voice could probably describe. But for the writer of this collection of poems, the passage of time has probably blurred some negative history. It is said that over extended periods of time, we tend to repress or selectively forget the bad.

Probably that happened here.

The use of the title "Growing Up In My Little Italy" is a liberty I have taken with the poetry and it coincides with the Little Italy project which first adapted "Little Italy" for its purposes. To me, its reference is synonymous with the Hill or the Northside. Although the name Little Italy was not in vogue during the period portrayed, its use is well justified by its similarities to a host of other Little Italies throughout the country. Name any large city in the USA and you will likely find an Italian enclave that resembles our Little Italy. I have also used the title "The Hill" interchangeably with the Northside or the Nob, although that name was more commonly used by non-residents.

The tone of the poems that follow is happy and nostalgic – a "good old days" theme. They are intended for those who live on the Northside or its environs, as well as for those who have moved away, but carry fond memories of days long past. They are dedicated particularly to those residents, both native Italians and Italian-Americans on the Hill, past and present, and invite them to hear and to read in part what neighborhoods were like for their parents and grandparents in an era several decades ago. Because America is a melting pot of cultures, it is a story that should be told, preserved, and cherished.

In the collection of poems, there are some which are not significantly related to the theme. They are the nostalgic thoughts and reflections of one Northside octogenarian as he comes to view his life in the twilight of his years.

The Tammetta Family, 1933

I. *Northside Endicott -*
The Place and the People

From the Other Side of the Tracks

A Walk Up The Hill

On the Hill or Nob as it was known
we had our own space, our own geography
beginning with North Street
northward past the underpass
and Erie railroad tracks
which we were on the other side of
physically and literally,
up Oak Hill Ave.
past the dingy bars
with their vacant grimy look
and the pervasive tannery smell
and by stark contrast the Battaglini bakery
that still exists today, and with it
the exquisite aroma of fresh bread baking.

It was a gradual ascent
with a glut of hilly side streets
Odell Ave. and Watson Blvd.
with side trips to the Bocce courts on Hill Ave.
then to Squires Ave. and Pearl's Bakery
where a dime got you
a bag of yesterday's fried cakes
then back up Oak Hill
past the Oaks Inn, a pizzeria at that time
that today remains a gourmet ristorante
to the park and carousel.
And in that narrow lane
between the park and the bar next door,
now a parking lot,

the spiedie came of age -
roasted chunks of barbecued lamb
sizzling on that tiny charcoal grill
with each splash of that secret marinade,
fresh Spring lamb
its grade now unattainable
the smokey fragrance
enticing anyone to resist at 10 cents a skewer.
And the question of the origin of the spiedie
contested to this day.

Our Neighborhoods

The ethnicity of our neighborhood was primarily Italian
but that influence weakened
as one headed eastward
where neighborhoods became more Eastern European.
The crisscrossing streets became our neighborhoods
where first-generation kids identified with their streets.
You were an Oak Hiller or Odeller
and you played and competed
against those streets on vacant corner lots
mainly football, as I recall
because we were a football town.
It was Robble vs. Bermond
or Oak Hill vs. Murphy
pure sandlot
with no adults or referees to supervise
no interfering whiny parents
or soccer moms
to second guess a call.

Touch Football or Pee Wee, as we called it
was our Fall thing on my street.
Trees or lamposts were the goals,
off sides, a flower bed.
Captains chose up sides
the bigger players chosen first,
an obvious Darwinian chose
as the bigger usually produced,
best able to block or catch a pass
and the last were usually younger or undersized.
Sure, some hard feelings for them
but they lived with it, grew up and got better.

Each street had its own distinction.
To me, Odell was a tough street.
A gang often took over the lower corner,
down from the Julian Block and
adjacent to St. Anthony's church.
Territorial and itching for action
they were not friendly to trespassers.
Here comes tough, tiny Joe Olivieri,
then the Testani brothers.
I would avoid that corner like the plague.

The Hill itself was rumored to be dangerous
after dark
by some of the South Side community.
Not wise to cross
those railroad tracks at night
if you weren't a resident
they'd warn you.
No doubt, part of the
prevailing stereotype baggage
we Italians carried at that time.

The Residents

The Hill had its own elites,
the undertaker, Tony DeMarco,
as I recall him
hatless, dressed in black
and directing funeral traffic.
Fr. Lynch, the Irish priest revered by all.
And the Italian E.J. doctor, Dr. Maggiore
who made house calls,
not a resident but known to all
and respected for his common touch.
He played a horn and marched
in church parades.

And there were those Damon Runyon types
generous, hard drinking
good-hearted sports,
with their Cadillacs
and spiffy clothes
some rumored to be connected
unintimidated by authority,
never turn you down for a favor
always good for a drink
and quick to pick up a tab,
often at the Northside Social Club.
And the sports icon of that era
an idol to kids and adults alike
Joltin' Joe Matisi, the heavyweight
with a blockbluster punch
who almost made it to the top.

And then there were the other
minor personalities
colorful factory working types and their children
poor but generous and fun loving
where family was primary.
They did not seek approval
or bow to the status quo
rather, they ignored the establishment
and created their own lifestyles.
They had their nicknames
(I dare not personalize)
strange contorted tongue twisting sounds
blends of foods
facial features or body types
or fractured Italian surnames.
How uncertain when to use them
if you met some old respectable acquaintance
with the passing of the years.
Would they be embarrassed if you did?

Analysis

The Italian uniqueness
was the ability to
see through pretension
with a disdain of titles and authority
that sometimes had negative consequences.
They bent rules
that to them seemed arbitrary
and had a weakness
with structure and order
often making choices
based on emotions
and often capricious.

How to unravel the Italian psyche
to explain these behaviors?
A passive aggressive resistance to authority
based on an oppressive
history as immigrants?
An inherited temperament?
Or a gene that won't suffer fools?
And while their actions
were occasionally maddening,
they never were boring
and most often a hoot!

Street Corner Society

We were a street corner society
especially under lamposts after dark
where the circle of light
became our safety zone,
where talk or games took up our night.
Our play equipment
consisted of rocks, sticks, cans,
wadded newspapers with jar rubbers
and for winter sports
cardboard boxes for sledding
and curtain rods for skiing
often on the slope
that currently is occupied
by the St. Anthony Church.

It was on that corner
that you got your sex education
through the storied adventures
of your older peers
(real or imagined),
or were initiated
in one type of male coming of age ritual
(if you lived in my neighborhood)
when your pants were forcibly removed
and hung up on a tree.
Go figure and retrieve.
The corner became a staging point
where strategies were concocted
for raiding nearby fruit trees

or harassing pesky neighbors,
selecting those most likely
to be aroused and give chase.

While I lived a scant 50 yds.
from the corner of Robble Ave. and Pine St.,
when talk turned to werewolves
or the Malocchio (evil eye)
said to be possessed by old Mrs. C
who lived in our neighborhood,
I dared not venture home alone
beyond the safety of that corner lamp-post.

To the believers,
a bad headache
could be attributed to the Malocchio.
And a horn-like amulet
worn as a necklace
by some old southern Italians
would protect you.
Today it is a popular jewelry piece
worn by Italians
as a sentimental artifact.

The Woods Around Us

To the north and to the west
from the rim of a bowl
looking downward toward the Hill
were woods where we hiked and we berried
hunted birds with our BB guns
and gathered hickory nuts.
Trudging up the hill to these woody playgrounds
we would pass a herd of goats,
raised as a family sideline, for some
and an economic necessity.
They were tended by our busy friends
shepherds for that day
and stuck in the hot summer sun
how envious they seemed of us at play.

And beyond the rim and further west
the fields would sharply drop
down Danger Hill
and take you to the Crick
to the Suckers Hole or the Bend
names we gave our special water holes
and never Nanticoke Creek
which it really was.
It was here we fished or swam all day
in pools of translucent green
before they became polluted,
then the crawl
back up Danger Hill
and home, and totally wasted.

Church field days were held at one lofty point
overlooking the entire Valley
and just above the shrine of our patron saint,
now an upscale residential site
sedate and sterile.
It stands in contrast to the shouts and music
drifting downward on that special day in June
la Festa di Sant'Antonio.
How is it that
after 70 years or so
I can still see Mr. Lockett's smiling face
squeezing his Concertina?

Angelo Lockett

The Sons of Italy Lodge

What I remember most of the Lodge
as the Sons of Italy was called
was that my father went there
most weekday nights
a 7PM to 9PM routine
with never any objections from my mom.
It was usually talk or a friendly game of Briscola
where drinks were stakes
never overdone or drinking to excess.
Winners decided who would drink.
Occasionally my father would announce at home
"Patsy sent me dry tonight,"
his choice as a winner.
Disappointment was the implication
since they were the best of friends.
And when an official meeting of the Lodge took place
the word was spread by mouth "7 o'clock meeting!"
It was uttered almost as a salutation
and repeated with mock urgency.

I remember the bar
the mild scent of beer
managed by the "Chief."
My dad would say,
"whatta you say, Chief,"
(his son would survive the Bataan Death March).
Being led into the bar
by one of my father's friends
meant that a treat was coming.

You would soon pick out a candy bar
most often the Hershey bar with almonds
wrapped in that shiny lead foil
which you occasionally extracted
and rolled into a tiny missile
for your rubber band wars.

Occasionally on Sunday mornings
and after the late High Mass for some
the Lodge became a stop
prior to the noon meal
once when some spender would step up
and buy the bar a drink
a quick stand-up routine
like a coffee bar,
a straight shot
Salute!
Then home to family by noon.

La Serenata

For birthdays or anniversaries
or at times for no special reason,
I remember the occasional Serenata,
a musical Neopolitan celebration
brought to your bedroom
usually a midnight surprise
and dedicated often to wives
of a close knit group of friends.

Suddenly out of the summer silence
a group of musician paesani would emerge
a mandolin, guitar, and vocalist
breaking into a Neopolitan love song
typically tearful and nostalgic and
awakening the neighborhood
but without hard feelings,
because it was an honor and a tribute
to hear or to be the recipient,
as serenades were carefully planned
a sign of respect and admiration
which in my case
my mother's quiet ways encouraged.
It lasted for but a few songs
and afterwards, the protocol encouraged
an inside invitation,
some freshmade cake and coffee
and perhaps an Anisette or two,
gladly offered for such an honor.

What did it signify,
this small gift of sentimentality
by this band of simple folks?
Was it a faded memory of their old world
when music and singing
were part of daily living
and a life they left behind?

In Italy, I recall the busses and the car rides
when singing was a given
and minutes after boarding
as if on cue and without announcement
like some acapella choir,
riders would break into a native song
and cheerfully pass the time.

Where are you now when we need you
you long departed serenaders
when a Serenata today
might be staged for hire,
professional and more skillful perhaps,
but devoid of soul
which these simple men imparted?
Was something missing in their lives
which they treasured and tried to recreate
to preserve and to pass on
to a younger generation
and show what was in their hearts?

Can you conceivably imagine
a Serenata brought to you by friends today
under your bedroom window
on a starry summer night?

Wolfing

Our street corner
bordered a wooded area
known as Pizur's woods
with its own lover's lane.
And when passing cars
selected a northward turn
from our corner
into the black of night,
we suspected its eventual destination.

And after being bored with talk,
we planned our next diversion – wolfing,
our word for spying on lovers
in various stages of romance.
In a word, we became Peeping Toms.

After a target was selected
and after our eyes
became accustomed to the darkness
and stalking stealthily toward our prey
like those giant cats
on National Geographic
to the rear window
of the hapless victims inside,
and after sensing
the precise strategic moment
we would give charge,
stomp on running boards and bumpers
and scatter into the night!

September Tomatoes

Tomato gardens were as common on the Hill as the
front lawn. When you asked an old southern Italian
about the best time to plant tomatoes, he'd deliberate
momentarily and then announce with solemnity, an
exact day of the month, depending, of course, on the
position of the moon.

We plucked what remained of them
from bearded thickened vines
tomatoes the color of dead flesh
or sickly pink
sagging and sexual
yielding to the touch and dropping
or fiercely resistant
the haggard vines were doomed for compost.

The September sun was fake
bright but tepid
couldn't finish what it started in July
when tiny knobs
first peered through yellow buds.

In August, they hung patiently
but cool nights
and later hard September rains
left them pale and sickly.
So we triaged.
And like little preemies
we incubated them in baskets
each wrapped in a paper blanket
and set them in a darkened corner.
Here they thrived
snuggling for life and color
then glowed to rosey red.

The Shack

For street members only
a shack was your home
away from home.
It was a hideaway
a clubhouse retreat
a few boards slapped together
in someone's backyard –
wood, tin, wire, cardboard
as long as it crudely resembled
four walls and a roof
and could stand on its own.
It was not to be taken lightly
and almost institutionalized
like some secret society.
It guaranteed privacy and exclusivity
members only stuff.
Where else could you get away from it all
swap stories
and maybe grab a smoke?

During the doldrum days of summer
scrap collecting became a sideline –
rags, paper, copper, brass and aluminum
had value even before the war.
We would stash the stuff
in our shack,
and when a sufficient amount
was accumulated
and carefully bundled,
off we went to Mr. Sementelli's garage
who would weigh the stuff
and reward us with a few coins.

Little Italy

Things are different on the Hill today
gentrified, the noisy factories are gone
the ethnic pool more varied
becoming artsy
with cabarets, outdoor cafes and coffee bars,
another Little Italy in the making.
While new blood shapes the past
some old blood will never leave the Hill
its memories or their roots.

So there you have my snapshots
3 x 5 glossy black and whites
a mini-view of life
as I recall it
at a time when we were young.
You may touch them up
or talk them up
or even take your own,
but then store them in a special place
to keep the memory safe
to remind you of those golden years
with pictures that do not lie
and realize your good fortune
in knowing that you were there.

Dr. M. Maggiore
Photo: The Broome Co. Historical Society

**Camille Paglia,
College Graduation**
Photo: The Broome Co. Historical Society

1947 NORTHSIDE SOCIAL CLUB FOOTBALL CLUB
Preparing to travel to a game in Stuart, Florida
Kneeling: ?, Joe Minni, Dick Conti, Jimmy George, Bob Guarnieri, Neish Longo, Pat Salammie
Standing: Dino Santacrose, Lou Gimmie, Art Daglio, Spill Battista, Paul Cardone, Slim Sylvester, Pat De Santis,
Ray Minni, Pat Sergi, Dick Marino, Joe Pisani, Joe Cordi, Ugo D"Aloisio, Mike Coppala, Chuck Alio, Bob Kropp

Aurora Tammettta, 1924

Washington Avenue, 1948

GRASSI BROS.
COSMO DANNY FRANK JOHN MONROE
1938

24

The old Tedeschi Market, present day

Sons of Italy building, present day

Can you match any of these names with the faces? **Antonelli, Monforte, Corino, Ferris, Minnie, Caforio, Pasalida, Jimmy The Greek, Fucci, Rotunno, Luizzi, Rizzi, De Santis, Piccirilli, Anz, Sciappia, Parisella St. Anthony Park, 1936.**

Hillside Center Library, Odell Avenue, 1930's

St. Anthony Park, 1934

Jimmy Lockett, Jim Fiori, Mondo Cordlione, Peter Julian, Rudy Testani, Ange Longo, Joe Oliveri, Joe Berri, Frank Marcocci, Ange Pozzi, Nick Rano, Nondo Bernard, Sam Lupo, Picciano, Tony Olevano, Signorelli, Father Lynch, Jimmy Fiori, Pat Fiorelli, Armand Olevano, Larry Minni, Peter Greco, Louie Picciano, Al Calleo, Hector Colonna, Sparky Lockett, Joe Convertino, Sam Fargnoli, Tom Crescente, Mike Maggi, Jim Arcangeli, Berni Battaglini, Rudy Veruto, Tony Lannone, Dave Battaglini, Paglia, Jr. Picciano, Dino Santacrose, Joe Pisani, Mangini, Mike Coppola, Bob Corino, Al Marcocci, Joe "Endwell" Convertino, Vito Longo, Mano Irnelli, Paglia, Checko Musso, John Musa, Larry Testani, Red Longo, Vic Lacatena, Mike Quartararo, DeStefano, Nick DeBenedittis, Benny Musso, Nick Rano.

11. *Our Church and Cemetery*

Father Geremia, 1930's

Father Gafney, 1944

Father Monteleone, 1950's

Photo: The Broome Co. Historical Society

Dedication - St. Anthony's Church, 1942

Calvary Cemetary

Old St. Anthony's
(with apologies to Andy Mancini)

The old church stands
kitty corner from the Lodge
as we call the Sons of Italy clubhouse
a stubborn artifact
made over and modernized
into a corporate office
with patchy touches,
some colored glass
and a business logo,
a facelift that fails
like one for some aging contessa
faded and worn
trying to make her what she's not.
Because old St. Anthony's will always be
a church to me.
A memorial for departed friends
and former neighbors
who once prayed and worshipped there.
Where births and deaths were celebrated,
where Fr. Geremia droned on in a sing-song monotone
praying as in some Far Eastern chant.
Ghosts must still linger in what remains of the
organ loft,
spirits that won't be exorcised,
all remnants of our bittersweet past.

It was in that darkened basement
where I studied the Catechism
lined against the wall,
memorizing and preparing to recite in rote

to the waiting teacher priest
the fundamentals of our faith
from "who made the world"
to regurgitations of venial and mortal sins,
Extreme Unction and the Immaculate Conception.

It was in this church
we experienced rites of First Communion
and later Confirmation
when the Bishop came from Syracuse.
And in an altar ritual
which we nervously awaited,
as predicted by your elders,
he might ask you a question on your faith
followed by the confirming slap
that made the rite complete.
But the frosting on this blessed event
was the anticipated wrist watch –
your Confirmation gift
as presented by your sponsor.

Corporate offices, (formerly St. Anthony's)

Saturday Confession

There was Saturday confession
leaving a sun-filled afternoon at play
to enter the hush of a somber, darkened church
where mounted Saints looked down at us
in imagined condemnation
as we prepared ourselves
and examined our consciences
as we were trained
and tallied up our sins.

The dual lines to each confessional
said it all regarding favored priests,
the longer line well worth the wait
when the reprimand was spared
and your penance was light –
(three Our Fathers and three Hail Marys).

Time hung heavy in the empty church
silence broken at intervals
by the slamming echos of the confessional screen.
And when it was over
how light you felt when you stepped out
to be greeted by the nervous next-in-line.
Your burden lifted for another month.

St. Anthony's, today

The Stations Book

Most vivid and unforgettable
of all the early church years
was the memory and my experience
as a six year old
during the Easter season
when two aunts escorted me
to the church rectory
to obtain a Stations prayer book
used for Friday Lenten services.

Fr. Lynch responded kindly and amused
looked down at me and questioned
my ability to read
to which I gave him my assurance
(although I was not quite yet a reader).
He pointed to a word and asked what it said
and from my lips and with a word
I had never seen before,
out came "Jesus,"
And to this day I will never forget
or will I ever comprehend
the mystery of that brief encounter
when through some power
or mystical intervention,
I was able to read the word "Jesus."

Calvary Cemetery Revisited

There is a lower section of Calvary Cemetery in
Johnson City that contains the graves of many
immigrant Italian Americans who lived on Endicott's
Northside, including my father. This poem remembers
them and their lives and fantasizes their final resting
place.

In death they rest together.
In life they were neighbors on the Hill.
Clustered and segregated
by the Hill itself
trudging homeward daily
from noisy factory destinations
the scent of leather soaked in what they wore.

Factory whistles ticked out their days.
No shrill bells were these
but thundering, bellowing blasts
that boomed the start and close of day
echoing throughout the Valley
with commanding authority.

We were a boom town
during the war years
and never more obvious
then in the summer months
when the clatter and smells
of shoemaking at all stages
seemed magnified
spilling from the open grimy windows of workers
with jobs such as
edge trimmers, stitchers, or bedlasters.

Then a generation passed.
Life evolved.
The war was over
work grew leaner
the hills grew steeper
pulses weakened
and they crossed over
and found rest
in a sunnier flowered place.

Here they remain remarkably together
old friends at arms reach
no hills to climb
or clocks to punch
no whistles to jar them from their sleep.

Now their names are etched in stone
their permanence assured.
They rest throughout the day
and when the flower tenders leave,
through dried out lips
they call up old friends
with birdlike whistles
from Old World days
each whistle special to his town –
"Bruno" "Patsy" "Ernesto!"
And with a new arrival
they would say, "He's the last of our bunch, you know,"
as he brought news of changes on the Hill.

They talk through moonlit nights
of life so quickly passed
recall old ghostly serenades
for lovers now at peace.
They cling to family memories
their precious legacy
and talk and talk
until the sun comes up
and brightens up their names.

III. *Our Schools*

The old Northside School, present day

Early Grades - The Northside School

Where are you now my grade school teachers
from those post-depression days?
We judged you carefully
and planted labels and gave you names
that defined you in our eyes,
usually nice or mean,
occasionally qualifying or embellishing
but generally straightforward
in either black or white terms.
And with stirring hormones, forgive us
peceived a sexual slant
to any of your body language
which our imaginations would dream.

It was in the Kindergarten band
where I clanged the bells
that task for drones
when teacher's pets were the drummers
or the tambouriners,
kids like Peppy Colamarino.
And who can forget Mrs. Davidson
that Kindergarten pseudo mom
whose big heart and kindness
matched her ample girth?

Report Cards and Promotion

First grade introduced "port cards" as we called them
when achievement would be quantified
official statements for our parents.
My first "red mark" came in the second grade.
Report cards pulled no punches.
Failing grades jumped out and were recorded
in bright red ink.
No qualifiers like "needs improvement" or
"needs to spend time more wisely."
Failure was unequivocal and clearly "failure."

And the apprehension of that last day of school
when final port cards were distributed
along with verdicts on promotion.
Tomorrow came the Teddy Bear haircut
always cooler for the summer
and for the more daring, the "baldy,"
sheared to the skin.

But today this final day would be endured.
Selective memory recalls a classic June day
oppressive heat, humidity, cloudless skies,
a stirring breeze
summer sounds
and the smells of new mown grass
wafting through open windows
dressed up boys and girls with stiffened postures
with some awaiting the blackest news –
non-promotion, grade retention - failure!

And how the word would spread.
And with the repeated failure for some
more ominous was the threat of "dumb school,"
our unfortunate term for transfer to special education
to the Broad St. school downtown.
For others, there was the Honor Roll
when an average of 90 and above
got your name in the Endicott Daily Bulletin
our own Village newspaper
as well as embellished in a multi-colored
blackboard display (we didn't call them chalk boards)
there to remain carefully shielded for at least a month.

The Middle Grades

How special it was to be your teacher's helper
to wash the blackboards
or clap the erasers
or fill the inkwells after school.
It was okay to talk or laugh out loud.
Your teacher was a different person after hours.
You were like a peer and
she talked to you like one.

After a string of female teachers
your first male teacher was a rite of passage
a transition figure to the upper grades
and an expectation of less monkey business
and possibly more meanness
though that term began to fade
as we approached the Junior High.
The knuckled fist of Mr. Brace
was our first reminder that
times indeed were changing.
His knuckle would grind against your scalp
when things went wrong.
Knuckle pressure depended on the crime
either learning or behavior (or both).

Our Principal

He was a sentinel on the playground
"a silent watchman" as those old link fences quietly
warned,
a no nonsense figure – the wool topcoat
the Stetson, the gloves and the flannel scarf
our first brush with real authority,
standing aside, scanning, troubleshooting.
Not a chatty friendly sort, but cooly efficient
with an occasional shrug or hitch of the shoulders
a tic perhaps,
but we had our own explanations.

At noon recess, he monitored the playground.
One Fall pastime was "scrambling."
A chosen pair of boys was selected
to kick a football from the field
to an eager mob of receivers
the lucky catcher to be rewarded
with the prize of kicking back the leather nugget.
While some of us owned a football
we sternly warned others not to kick it
less it get ruined or go shapeless
and back to footballs made of
wadded newspapers wrapped with jar rubbers
which some kids learned to kick
a perfect spiral.

So here we could kick with wild abandon.
How sweet it was!
And often a battle would ensue
on that hard pan playground
when two sets of arms would claim the prize
to be settled by a frenzied bout
of rolling bodies and wrenching arms
that might extract that treasure from one bony grip,
resolved, if necessary, by Mr. Woodard himself.
Tomorrow we would check the posted list
for the envied pair of kickers
assigned for that day.

School Dismissal

For noon or afternoon dismissal
Mr. Woodard played parade master
as we lined the darkened halls
awaiting the signal to advance
(no talking please)
and when all was hushed and orderly
with the Victrola cranked to max,
down dropped the stylus
upon that charcoal disc
and from the bowels of that wooden box
out scratched "The Stars and Stripes Forever."
And with military aplomb, we picked up the cadence
and exited the building
with Mr. Woodard's approval.

De Witt Woodard, principal

Crushes

The inevitable first teacher's crush
came in the fourth grade.
How refined and elegant Ms. Porter seemed
soft spoken and classily dressed
pretty and fragrant,
her perfume scent lingering momentarily
as she passed your desk.

And Sylvia, your first school girl crush.
That banana curled, dark skinned beauty,
perfect teeth and posture – perfect everything!
Her outfits were impeccably starched.
I never dared to approach or confront her
too scared to say hello.
How did the word get out
that brought those terrible taunts –
and those sing-song ditties
that never seemed to end
and laid the secret bare?
Dominick "Tomato" loves so-and-so, so-and-so.
How excruciatingly embarrassing!

The Rubber Tube

And then there was the rubber tube
a last ditch tactic
of corporal punishment
intended for those incorrigibles
for whom all diplomacy or counseling failed,
even after the dreaded home report.
It was a tube – not a paddle or a belt
but actually a tube?
It was referred to in hushed tones
as in some secret ancient rite
imposed in the inner sanctum
of the Principal's office.
It was never overplayed
or spoken openly or used to threaten,
but quietly deployed with stern efficiency
when the need was clear.
What was it really like?
How much did it hurt?
I never experienced it or knew or heard
a victim's dread description of that moment.
But the word got out.
"He got the rubber tooh!"
As we called it in our lexicon of fractured phrases.
How awesome! How terrifying!
No further need be said.
The grapevine did the rest
as did his parents
when the news reached home.

Music Class

About this time, Ms. Kessler taught us singing.
She wore those horn-rimmed glasses
her hair a pulled bun
delicate manicured hands
sophisticated and Waspy,
leading us in "My Country Tis of Thee."
And we would sing it for Mr. Gillespie
the big music honcho from downtown
who occasionally visited at assembly.
And he would remind us that the emphasis was on
"thee"
in my "My Country Tis of Thee"
and tell us how fortunate
we Italian kids were
with our musical heritage
that from the open windows
as he rode up the hill,
he would hear some lovely Italian arias.

Classroom Talk

We never put our coats or sweaters on
we put our "wraps" on
which were always in the "cloak room."
We never asked to use the lavatory,
it was always the "basement."
And mid-morning recess was our
"basement period."
And if attendance was your problem
it was the "tune" officer who called.
And for casual writing,
we would always use "scrap" paper.
And should you be munching on some goodie
which you didn't care to share
you would protect your treat
by shouting "no hags!"
On the other hand
you knew you were entitled to a bite
if you beat them to the punch with
"Haggies!!"

Palmer Method Writing

How envious I was of
(usually) girls who made such
perfect ovals and push-pulls
with the Palmer Method Program,
those long abandoned exercises
designed to improve your penmanship.
"Arms only" please
as you tried to execute your ovals
to look like a perfect slinky.
And those vertical push-pulls
looking like a brush haircut on paper
so easy with flicking fingers
which you tried when teacher wasn't looking
but always redirected and reminded
that it was a full arm movement please
that led to perfect writing.
But it was quite a stretch to me
that ovals and push-pulls
could make a better writer.
Or that full arm thrusts
was the key to forming perfect letters
like those in the Palmer Method Handbook.

Penny Candy

And how about penny candy
from Rose's or Pezzola's candy stores
adjacent to the school?
We would stock up on Chum Gum (5 sticks per cent)
or hats, tar babies, licorice twists (red or black)
Tootsie Rolls and those teeth-sticking gummy green
leaves.
For quality stuff, there were Mary Janes,
pricey at three for a cent
compared to those licorice hats at 15 per penny.
Hats became a time consuming purchase
counted carefully one by one by Mr. Rose
during a rushy noon hour.

And when time permitted
there was the jaw breaker
that rock-like golf ball jumbo
that barely fit your mouth.
With nonchalance, we would tuck it in one cheek
that swelled like one bad toothache
and let the juices trickle
in one sweet slow release
(unless you got a hot and peppery one).
No chewy molar sticking problem here,
good for an hour easy
a bit pricey at one cent
but overall a good deal.
And when you couldn't hide it
when school would soon resume
you would doggie bag it til later
and suck and suck until it disappeared.

Playing Alleys

In favorable weather we played alleys,
our word for marbles (don't ask why).
On a dirt surface, usually on the school playground
we scratched the circle.
Each player placed an alley inside the pot
and from a designated line
approached the circle with his shooter
and tried to blast the alleys from the pot
which then became his prize to keep.
"Outsets or insets" were cries before some shots
technicalities of the game.
You could use a "steelie" for your shooter
if you so desired.
A steelie was a steel ball bearing
which was heavier and with some advantages.
No "migs" allowed (inferior wooden imitations).
You might choose a jumbo shooter
which could bowl over other alleys
but it was an easy target
to be hit by other players
which removed you from that round
and forfeited your winnings.
Some wag would occasionally use a BB
impossible to hit
but almost impossible to shoot.

In cold or muddy weather
we improvised a glove
with cutoff fingers that protected knuckles
from a wet or frozen surface.
And when the season started
you might be "corps" with another friend
which became a season's partnership.
You and your partner
both went your separate ways
and played your separate games
but you pooled your wins or losses
and divided up the booty
at the season's end.
Games with hot shots were avoided.
Their reputations were legend on the streets,
like Tony Salamida or May-May Roma.
You didn't stand a chance!

It was so rewarding at home
to run your fingers through your alleys
especially those you won,
those pure translucent crystals
and the clicking spectacle
of all those glassy colors.
That "popeye" alley
with red and white designs
like the markings on the moon.

Going To School Downtown

Entering the 8th grade
meant a transfer downtown
to the Henry B. Endicott Junior High School
on Jackson Avenue
since our little school
ran out of space after the 7th grade.
Seemed simple enough
except that "downtown"
was exotic and culturally different enough
from our insular world
to almost suggest one needed a passport.
Everything special was downtown –
the shops, the parks, the movies
and the "Avenue" – a cabaret.

But school downtown every day?
Quite a leap.
And to rub shoulders each day
with kids outside our own space
who were known to us as "Americans"
was a further leap indeed.

From a boy perspective
and as school continued
we learned to give special names to "them"
sotto voce.
And they had in turn had special names for "us"
sotto voce.
Somehow cake eaters or towners
branded them as sissy types
less macho than us

although the word "macho"
was not Americanized at that time.
And for us, the usual ethnic labels applied.

But how quickly our macho bubble
burst in the classroom
when kids with last names like
Rogers, Bennett, or Burton
(no ending vowels?)
seemed smarter and more verbal,
cooler, more sophisticated and articulate
than us
with grades and honors as proof.

But with time and exposure
we surfaced,
our rough edges less obvious
emerging as students, many superior
and holding our own.

But the test of inclusion into their circles
lay outside of the classroom
where friendships and alliances blossomed.
It was in the hallways and playgrounds
and events extra-curricular,
it was here where pretenses were dropped.
We knew we belonged
when put downs were open
when name calling was openly exchanged,
when slurs were delivered
full faced and with laughter,
then we knew we arrived.

School Lunch Hour

Going to school downtown
meant getting there from home
with no school busses to haul us around.
And with two round trips per day
school became a 4-5 mile daily hike
up and down those hilly streets.
One option for lunch was brown bagging it
(which I occasionally did).
And in Junior High School
that meant an eggplant sandwich
while slugging down a warm Pepsi
sitting on an overturned soda case
in Baio's little grocery store.
Another option was the E. J. Diner
where for 20 cents
you were treated to a three-course dinner
and occasionally taken up by many of us.

In High School I recall Fred's Hamburg Heaven
on the Avenue.
On one Friday, having lunch there
I ordered something I never had before
or ever heard of – a cheesburger.
It was Friday
and with the meat thing
for Catholics at that time,
I thought it was a special type cheese sandwich.
I ate it and discovered hamburg.
Then the pangs of guilt began.
Who ever heard of cheese on hamburg?

The last lunch option
God forbid
was the school cafeteria.
But of all of my years in public school,
I never saw the inside of a school cafeteria.
What exactly was it
about eating your own food
that made all that walking worthwhile?

Early Morning Shop

And for the men among us
who can forget those pitch black
early morning shop classes
at the U.E. High School?
They were part of what was called
the Technical Program
an elite vocational sequence
light years ahead
of the 9th grade woodshop program
where a semester project
was the wooden buzzer.

This was a metal shop – serious stuff
a career builder
intended to prepare us
for a life at IBM,
the former computer giant
that originated in our little town
where employment there
became the pot of gold
at the end of the commencement rainbow.

The Technical Course was a quality one
but non-academic in emphasis
where counselors steered and placed
many of us first generation kids.
It was a more realistic choice
they believed
than the college entrance sequence,
simply not the best fit for us
except for a few shining stars

whom we alumni can name to this very day,
like Vince and Tony Vetrano.

And how this IBM carrot
was dangled before us
by our parents
who bought the dream
without reservation!
The best thing for their children
they believed,
a lifetime opportunity
in those gleaming antiseptic plants –
no piece work and with benefits and security
and the prestige!
It was a clear winner
over the shoe factory.
And while grateful
for that work opportunity
and its generous benefits
they simply aspired
something better for their children.

I recall the dreaded morning wakeup
for early shop
more like a midnight call to me.
Arising with my parents
and being driven to school
as they continued to work
being sure they "punched in" by 7AM
as affirmed by the morning whistle
hardly a whistle as we know one
booming throughout the factory town
like some deafening fog horn.

Shop classes were held
at the basement level
brightly lit up
in the early morning darkness
exposing it to me as an unfriendly alien place
with its smell of oil
and burning metal.
But for the mechanically inclined
and for those who grew up with tools,
it was a wondrous toyland
a grownup world
with sophisticated machinery
learning by doing,
absent the regimented desks
and the textbook emphasis.

But for me
the shop was a loathsome and threatening place
whose mechanical skills
in my klutzy upbringing
stopped at the level of a hammer.
Never was I able to attain
the genius level of my peers
who pounded and forged
and turned on a lathe
from pieces of raw steel
a marvelous metal screwdriver
gleaming, artful and knurled
so snug and polished
in your palm.

P.S. I transferred after the first semester.

IV. *Searching For Roots*

Who among us would not want to walk the streets
of his parents and grandparents in the old country?

My son, Peter and I, in Fondi

The Ancient Village

The old men sit and talk in dialect
and stare as we go by,
obviously strangers by our talk and dress.
They sit in café chairs and benches
in grey jackets, sweatered and scarved
despite the warming sun.
They talk with animation
of who knows what
and tease each other with their banter.

My father was one of them
an annual visitor in his later years.
I can hear him now badmouthing the street litter,
the kissing on the mouth,
the showoffs, heavily made-up older ladies,
this or that inefficiency
and how great things were back in the States.
When he was there, it was vice–versa.
It was "Mannagia l' America!"
Americans were corrupt
and Italy had no equal.
He left home at 17 for a new life
to be free, he always told me
but something Italian never changed
because as an old man he always cried
when he heard a Neopolitan love song.

My father was close to his mother
and he told me he almost hurt her
when he first when home and saw her

and hugged her
after 30 years or so.
And while he left home,
he never really grew up
seeing the world as a child.
Things were either black or white
and he was always about feelings and emotions
a pushover on discipline,
couldn't be mean
be nice, talk nice.
It got him in trouble later in life
passing out candy to children
from his car
when that was just not done.
But he never stopped
even when the police warned him
because he loved children
and he felt good doing it.
So why should he stop?
I knew he loved me as a boy
but later in life
after my mother died and he grew bitter
and when I didn't meet his expectations,
I'm not sure he even liked me.

Street Life In Fondi

The cobbled streets are worn and glassy
very Roman and built for chariots,
where my grandfather, Domenico,
took his daily passeggiata
on the Viale della Libertá
past the family cantina
and where my father told me
he and his boyhood chum
picked up cigarette butts there
and on the road to Sperlonga.

He was sort of a hell raiser,
never could stay put
even as an old timer.
But his mother protected him
from a sterner father
like he protected and overprotected me.

The old men still play cards
in front of café bars,
their wine glasses nearly empty.
And children still
chase pigeons in the piazza
in their knee socks,
buckled shoes, and Bennetton colors,
with Mamma shadowing right behind
like many Italian mothers
within reach of any child
even as they turn forty

Like him we visit and keep returning
to the ancient town,
reliving the past
searching for roots
and trying to go home again
(if anyone can ever go home again).

The town takes on an outward sprawl
new construction at its edges
wood replacing stone.
But the center remains unchanged,
a fortress of stone, brick, and ancient walls
that seem impenetrable
as is anyone could dislodge
that steel-like Roman mortar.

Ettore who ran the gelato shop is dead
as is his English-speaking wife
we would desperately seek
just to hear some English
and some small talk from a native.
And so is Uncle Vincenzo dead,
always dressed up and natty
as he went to work each day
until he was ninety.

Birds still swoop and dive in the piazza
where the ancient Castello Baronale
lights up at night
and the little boys who played there
like my father
now line the benches
at talky old men.

Not much has changed on the Corso d' Italia.
It's siesta time at mid-day
and the passegiata,
that late afternoon promenade,
that mating game of elegantly dressed
and bejeweled ladies
continues unfailingly.

Not much goes on at church –
no socials, dinners, or ice cream fests.
At Sunday Mass,
men are few and far between
except on religious holidays
when show and spectacle are expected,
then each one looks his pious best.

Ironically, life is busiest at the cemetery
at one end of town
with a thriving florist on the premises.
It is gated, newly paved and carefully landscaped
with above ground burials,
concrete walls
with six foot rectangular openings
stacked cubicles of emptiness
so many crypts waiting to be filled.
Here, young looking widows
keep scurrying, cleaning and scrubbing,
toting pitchers of water
placing fresh flowers (always fresh flowers)
before smiling faces of loved ones
macabre photo I.D.'s
portraits frozen in crystal and stone.

The Family

Thirty-five summers ago
when we first visited,
life centered at the beach.
And like some privileged family
which they were,
we had our own space
our private mini-beach.
We knew the rules.
Our days were measured by the table.
Food was primary
and when the clock struck one
we knew where we should be.
Be late for the noon meal
and face the boss, my father's sister
the oldest family survivor
who reigned as matriarch,
who with firm but unspoken authority
remains unchallenged to this day.

Her kitchen table is loud.
Television blares in the background.
Someone is ridiculed.
An argument erupts.
Lucio belts out a song.
The food is critiqued.
The men nit-pick a problem.
They are never part of the cleanup.

Searching For Roots

We keep returning
to this pre-Roman village,
to the beach, the cobbled streets
to the timeless castle.
They all immutably remain.
Some old men are gone
giving up their seats
to the next generation and
finding their rest
in the seal of concrete.
Immutable as well
is the spirit of the people –
the gentilezza – the niceness
that behind all the bluster
the ridicule and loudness
is a kindness
and an incredible courtesy.

What draws us back and what are we seeking?
Our roots and renewal with family
and the memories.
But the lure is mysterious
tribal and clannish
perhaps a realization, like childhood
it will inevitably end.
But we are resigned to attrition.
Time takes its toll.
We all grow up and grow older.
The young move away.
People change, relationships change.

The matriarch or her successor
who will keep it together will change.

So we keep on returning
to renew the relationships
to enshrine our experiences
to lock in the memories
that we may never forget.

So that in the next generation
or in an epoch or two
we will look back with assurance
and a quiet conviction
that the family is vibrant,
that our roots have strength
and that our returns
were the best of all times.

Farmer's Market

Medieval Alleyway

Corso d' Italia

Piazza in Fondi

Castello Baronale

Lago di Fondi

V. Growing Up With Endicott-Johnson

Cut Number Two

Any story about the Northside would be incomplete without the effects of the Endicott-Johnson Shoe Corporation on the lives of its residents. Being a major employer to most individuals, its impact was total. Both my father and mother worked there.

"Which way E-J?" is a legendary expression supposedly attributed to immigrants searching for work in the early days of the company. Use of the phrase may be a myth but even as folklore it reflects how dependent they must have felt in a strange new environment seeking work. This writing is not meant to present a narrative of the industry and its economic implications or other demographics; rather it is a presentation of a series of recollections that touched our personal lives. It is limited and arbitrary and represents one person's experiences. Again, other residents could undoubtedly describe their own.

References to Endicott-Johnson will be referred to as E-J and to International Business Machines employees as IBMers, as they were commonly referred to.

I Remember...

The factory whistles
at 7 a.m., noon, and 4 p.m.
that almost blew you away
with their roaring reminders
of time to begin and
time to quit work.

The little carts
with standup drivers
of vats of smelly, jiggling hides
crisscrossing
from tannery to tannery
as you walked downtown.

The rancid tannery smells
we'd face heading downtown
hot putrid air
that could gag any stranger.
But to us it was just
"ho-hum, just a little smelly."

Buying E-J shoes on Thursdays
because there was a 10 percent discount
on that day only.

Ideal Hospital where I was born
where my tonsils were removed at age five
when to this day I can recall
the nightmare of crawling alligators
induced by the ether anesthesia.

I Remember...

The noon hour
when my parents returned
for their factory lunch
to feed me during my lunch hour.
My father always brought me
two huge jelly donuts
from his factory's
coffee wagon.

Spending a summer day at the factory
where my father worked
and all the attention
I received from all the ladies
in their aprons at work
at their stitching machines
looking up at me
and ogling a little boy
all dressed up and smiling.
But they couldn't get up or talk
or take the time to do so
since they were "piece" workers
and were paid according to "pieces"
they produced.

My dad at work
almost running and grabbing
bundles of leather pieces
that he stitched together as a "vamper"
and collecting the coupons attached.
He wasted zero time
because he was a piece worker too.

I Remember...

Helping my father count
his coupons after supper
which were turned in
weekly for his pay.
"Figuring my time"
as he called it.
Coupons were tied with a rubber band
and submitted with your time card.
($25.00 per week was a good week).

Most homes had no showers
so that a special treat for boys
was going to a tannery
to take one.
After winding your way
through a maze of
smelly vats and drying rooms,
we'd find some shower stalls
and no one stopped you
when you took one.

My father's reaction on hearing
he was eligible to buy an E-J house
after a lengthy waiting list
(cost some $3,800 total).
He was literally jumping for joy
one noon hour as he
broke the news to me.
It would take us out of our
two-bedroom walkup on Hill Avenue.

I Remember...

My reactions to the purchase and the moving
was a major disappointment.
I had to leave my Hill Avenue gang
the hangout at Marko's grocery store
and move away?
Vowing to return
to them every night,
I hardly ever saw them after moving.

The swimming pools at En-joie Park –
first the baby pool for toddlers
up to your knees
in tepid water
and usually with your mom.
Then came the big swimming pool
as we grew up
with "first" "second" and "high"
as we called the diving boards.
Quite a big deal
going off "high,"
a kind of transition to puberty.
It scared me to death
but I jumped and and with all the courage
I could muster
eventually dove blindly off the board.

I Remember...

The summer Sunday evening
band concerts at the park,
the gurgling of the filtering water
at the pool
with its smell of chlorine
as the day settled into twilight.

Frank Tei, directing
the Endicott-Johnson band
with Frank Ferris as emcee
singing the company song
in the opening number.
"Marching along together –
dum dee dum dee dum dum dum.
Making shoes together
dum dee dum dee dum dum dum.
You travel the East.
You travel the West.
Wherever you go they are the best –
Endicott-Johnson worker's shoes."
The program followed.

After the band concert
the short walk to Cappies
on Washington Avenue
for a peanut pop
with a Pepsi on the side.
The night was huge!

I Remember...

The E-J high tops
as they were called
leather boots
up to the knees
with a pocket on the side
for your jacknife.
Very cool.

The clod hoppers we bought
with the metal heel cleats
that made for
a good long wear
and a beautiful sound
in the hallways.

Babies born to E-J workers
in the 30's
received a ten dollar gold piece
and a pair of shoes
from the E-J Corporation.
They were known as
E-J babies.

Gold Piece for E-J Babies

I Remember...

The E-J Medical
at the end of Washington Avenue.
Register as you entered
and wait to be called.
The green colored lighting
the long darkened waiting room
and the overwhelming smell
of disinfectant
and a pervasive silence.
Then a door opened
and your name was called.
Your turn to see the doctor.
And it was all free.

The horrors of a dental visit for a filling.
The probing with the sharp curved pic
that sent you to the ceiling.
The cold air blast
on the problem tooth
and the drilling with
those wire drawn pulleys
(no novocaine of course)
with your head throbbing
with the grinding.
And the ecstasy
when the drilling stopped
as the dentist reached
for the silver filling.
(It was then I remembered
all those jelly donuts).

I Remember...

The summer days during the War
when they hired high school kids
to work part-time
in the factories.
My Dad got me into his factory
pushing bins of leather pieces
here and there.
How I hated being indoors
on beautiful summer days.

My father and his friends
talking up E-J jobs
the good and the bad.
A job was often categorized
"clean" or "dirty."
A clean job was a plus
but it never paid
like tannery jobs
which were dirty and harder
but best paying
and all time work.

Not many jobs
were paid by the hour
but what a sweet deal
it seemed to those who held them
like those IBMers.
I recall my Dad describing
how long he was able
to avoid the "toilet" and not lose time.

I Remember. . .

The complaint process
when workers had their gripes,
the ultimate appeal
was seeing Charlie Johnson –
not "Mr. Johnson" but "Charlie"
and he just happened
to be the President.

Entering and walking through
any factory
looking for a relative
or just wandering around.
There were few restrictions
or security people.
Some days we'd just
want to keep warm
on our way home from school.

My Mexican grandfather
trudging up to Robble Avenue
pulling a wagon of "American" bread
to feed his large family
which he bought at the E-J bakery
near the Sales Building
and wrapped in red and blue wax paper
with the E-J logo.

I Remember...

How IBMers were seen
as elite time workers and envied
wearing their white shirts and ties
and quite a contrast to most E-J factory people
in their factory garb
in comparison.

A man on the street perception
that IBMers were generally frugal people
or putting it more plainly "cheap,"
not prompt with bills and lousy tippers too.
Sour grapes? False stereotyping?
Of course, a gross overgeneralization
and a bit mean-spirited too.
But Italian-Americans
could probably write the book
on false stereotyping.
We carried our share.
But to many on the Hill,
this IBM thing was real.

My father never owned a checkbook.
All bills were paid in cash.
Head down to the nearest office
as soon as your bill came in
and hand over a fist full of dollars and coins.
Paying bills on time and being generous
were stereotypes E-J workers carried,
true or not.

E-J Shoe Worker

EJ Worker's Market   Stitching Room

82

Ideal Hospital

Babe Ruth and George F. Johnson

En-Joie Swimming Pool

Sales Building

George F. Johnson and his dog Bud

VI. *It's All About Retirement*

Image by Personal People

My Old Red Wagon

To all of my contemporaries, we are all old red wagons

That's my old red wagon
hanging in a darkened corner
dangling by its skinny arm
under old license plates
nailed to wooden beams.
Suspended among frayed ropes and broken wheels
old garden tools and useless scrap
heavy with the smell of old cars and gasoline,
it is a final resting place
of my old red wagon.

The words bleed through the rusty frame
as in an ancient frescoe
"Greyhound Flyer,"
a tinny and metallic relic
a model-T of wagons
bolted, sharp-edged and angular
with skinny wheels and dangling parts,
ignored in past garage sales.
It remains
an abandoned artifact
a gofer
a dirt hauler
a grocery carrier
a garage freak
a what have you.

Once it held a boy
bare legged and boney-kneed
who pumped and straddled the old wagon
into the sun and wind
across pot-holed roads
and bumpy sidewalks.

It rolled over chalky, innocent graffiti
and faded den keeper and hopscotch lines.
It raced with bikes
and towed ball bearing roller skaters.
It earned its name.
It was a Flyer.

Its successor is a noiseless wonder.
They call it a convenience carrier,
too good for the garage and
now a prissy playroom toy
with soft fat plastic flanks
colored yellow, strawberry pink or apple green
with cushy tires and sissy wooden side bars.
Could never fly a kid or race a bike
or last a minute on the street.
Where are you now when we need you most
my old red wagon?

The Silent Generation Revisited

We are that silent generation of the 50's
after the lost generation of World War I
and the Paris expatriates
between the Second World War and Vietnam
and before the sexual revolution of the 60's.
Unimaginative they called us
and unadventurous without burning causes.
We accepted the status quo
and would not rock the boat,
always just off the mark
of exciting times.

No valued veterans of any war
(we delayed the sexual revolution until our 30's).
On the fringes with the cyber world
that language too arcane for us
but simple for the young.
We opted for security
and careers that rewarded seniority.
Where are we now
and the rewards, if any,
for being goody boys and girls all those years?
Well, where we are is here,
we're still around
no lingering fire in our paunches
a flickering candle maybe,
while gutsy whiz-kids types
of a younger generation
lived their dream
took the jump and made small fortunes
when the market soared to flimsy heights

and eventually came to earth
as the world changed.

Where are we now we Silents?
Well, we're here, of course,
in between times as usual.
It's late afternoon but not quite twilight,
octogenarians with occasional senility
but still tuned in
measuring disease with numbers
exchanging scores on body readings
(daily organ recitals).
Words and names elude us
as memory vacillates.
Synapses still fire, but sluggishly.
We reason, but lose ourselves
when concepts fail
or when logic gets dead ended.

But physically, we carry on as usual
(or else we think we do).
Good that we can't see our stiffened selves
as in some video playback.
Actually, we're toddlers in reverse:
forging developmentally backwards
falling more often
crying more easily
short on patience
best at walking
and with fading libidos
best as voyeurs.

But we're still here
we borderline seniles
looking toward the next frontier.
And while the new frontier
is the solar system
and the universe beyond for some,
ours is locked within our selves.

To be lucid
to live without fear
to be at peace with ourselves
to grasp and to accept
the purpose of it all.
And to believe without equivocation
or to disbelieve as passionately,
that we are deathless.

It's All About Retirement

Today I watched my morning glories grow
up at least an inch from yesterday
the tender vines like baby fingers
squeezed and snuggled around my bamboo trellis
like on a daddy's finger.

The seed pods that you planted
need a jump start from the sun you know.
You've got to scan the sun
each hour of the day
and visualize the arc
as it swings across the sky
and then you shift the pods
into the sun
whenever they hit shade.

And did you ever find the valve cap
for the tire you were pumping?
It must have rolled away
as you moved the bike around.
The tire could deflate, you know
and make it hard to peddle.
So please keep looking.

Yes, I'll need the collar tab
that's missing since you stashed it,
(God knows where)
while maybe doing laundry?
You know we both hate wrinkled collars
so please search the bedroom one more time.
And the plastic caps you bought

for the chairs and table legs?
They're a quarter inch too small
and without them we could
scratch the kitchen floor.
So please exchange them at the mall.
And while you're there,
please get me another pair of laces
for my shoes (they're made of leather).
The others that you bought are just too short.
I'll just tie the two together.

We'll also need a second grapefruit knife
since ours is always missing
somewhere in the dishwasher
(as if it really needs a washing).
So get another, please,
you know they're serrated.

And if you're in a bath store
I noticed our shower curtain
has a hole without a ring,
so please get another.
I think they're plastic.

And remember that garage sales
will be listed in tomorrow's Classified.
We'll scout around the neighborhood
in case we see those book ends
or some cheaper paper backs.
If not, we'll check the sales cross town.

Sorry, Mrs. B, our friendly neighbor
the toothpick that you borrowed
didn't work to check your cake.
No, of course, you can keep it,
we have more.

Well, another day gone by.
How quickly they just fly.
If it's not one thing, it's another.
And people always ask us
how we manage all our time.
I just tell them
believe me, we're BUSY!

Analysis of Golf

It's all about the swing.
It's timing, tension, tempo and torque.
It's hands, hips, shoulders and butts.
It's length of arc
and width of arc (and maybe pray to
Joan of Arc).
It's parallel and lateral.
It's about the right side and the left side.
And the inside and the outside.
It's left heel up or left heel down.
It's a parallel line to the target line.
It's the weight here or the weight there.
It's 45 degrees here and 90 degrees there.
It's two inches here and four inches there.
It's preparation, position, and posture and pace.

You start with the stance.
Bend at the hips.
You're arms are loose.
Try a waggle if you choose.
It's weight on the right side,
the elbow tucked in
and the head real still.
Then the takeaway.
Start smooth – don't jerk (or be one).
From 9 o'clock to 4 o'clock,
first the shoulders, arms and hips.
You're at the top – don't rush.

Then reverse – come down,
the hips, shoulders, arms and hands,
behind the ball and inside line.
You whip your hands and
Pow! To the moon!
It's hard.

Wedding Vows and Beyond

As a test of our fidelity
when wedding vows are taken,
is it enough nowadays
to have and to hold
to love and to cherish
in sickness and in health
til death do us part?

For one thing, death does not part us
all that easily
as when those sacred vows were penned
and togetherness today
is considerably extended.
And what was known as sickness
is not so easily defined
since ailing bodies can be mended
with a pill, a valve, or a stent,
a booster cable for the heart
and we are restored to quasi health
to days approaching a century.

So with what wise counsel
or altered vows
if either would suffice
might some feeble centenarian
prepare the young and betrothed
to comprehend their promise
so eagerly recited
in the blush of summer
and to say with kindness and assurance
what only a mother could impress?

That love professed in June
must endure and be resilient
through December
when decades change the face of love
and even death is put on hold.

But maternal wisdom adds
while lifelong may lose its sheen,
the aging brain grows kinder
disdains a broken heart
and seeks to nurture
and be nurtured in return.

But in this extended caring
with fragile lives on hold,
in this loving hospice without pain
where living is to breathe
the sweet scent of memories;
in this prolonging and enduring
they may question the meaning of it all.

But in the end they will be blessed
for they will join that band of few
who choose to keep the promise
and more sublimely mate forever.

Composting

My compost is a summer stew
a smoldering mix of faded flowers
with lemon yellow Stella d'Oro
Spikey purple Russian Sage
and ruby red Clematis.

We scrapped bouquet remains
from flowery urns
into our moldy pile
along with emerald grasses gone to hay.
My lilies lasted but a day
bleached by summer heat
and sucked of chlorophyll
so into my stew they went.

Winter leaves defrosted in the early Spring
stuck fast in icy clumps and wet,
they dried and shriveled
when fed with sun and air
and crumbling went to soil,
a flower for my stew.
We added muddy coffee grounds
and seasoned with husks of nuts and eggs.

My meal was mulched by soaking rains
and cooked by August sun
it simmered through October
a potpourri of golden brown
full-flavored and enriched
by all that summer offered,
a feast of life and death.

We live but for a summer season
fleeting,
we thrive on sunny days
collect and remember what was best
into an attic trunk the relics go,
a battered toy
a wedding dress
a baby's shoes
a uniform
a yellowed newspaper
some brittle photos
and between the cover of a book of prayers
a dried out flower,
all mementoes of a lifetime summer
a trove of stuff
a hardy feast.

Country Dog

You show up regularly every morning
like the Tribune and the daily mail
staring through the storm door window
like you're waiting for a takeout;
those mournful, pleading, begging eyes
no whines or yelps
just that pathetic moon-faced look
(did I actually see a tear?)
that cries out
"Please help me, feed me!"
Why not don a mask and gun
and bark out "Gimme me all your scraps!"
And act like a real desperado
instead of a wet-nosed, wimpy Lab
which you are
and a country mutt to boot.

You wag your tail,
smack your lips
and salivate (drool to you)
when anyone approaches
like Pavlov's dog in that famous experiment
who did it with a bell,
as if you ever heard of Pavlov's dog.
A couple of handouts and you're gone.
Until tomorrow rolls around.

We all know you're a country dog
because, first of all
city dogs don't beg

and they don't eat table scraps.
Ever hear of leash laws
or a dog warden
or an invisible fence?
Wander off your space
and you get a nice little jolt.
And you know you scare people
when you travel around in packs
with your country pals
and bark at cars and bikers –
real redneck stuff.

I'll guess you don't even wear a collar
with your name and I.D.
Get caught and you'll end up in a shelter –
that's like jail to you.
They could put you up for adoption
or sell you.
You'll sleep on a concrete floor
instead of your hay-filled barn
next to the horses.
No more roaming the hills
on summer days
and cooling off in spring-fed lakes.

You know some city dogs have papers?
They're like fancy birth certificates.
Bet the only papers you know are wadded
and used for spanking.

City dogs get what we call pedicures.
They go every few weeks for nail clippings.
You're lucky you beat those rough asphalt
country roads with your calloused pads
and never need a clipping.

In the winter when its cold,
some city dogs wear coats
and even (don't laugh)
some apartment dogs wear little booties
for ice and snow.
You're lucky your coat is thick
and almost waterproof
from sleeping in a flimsy kennel
or in that airy broken down barn
in all kinds of weather.
Actually, in some ways
maybe you're kind of lucky.

You know how they train some city dogs?
They send them to Obedience School,
usually for dogs that don't mind,
bark at people and run off
and do all the things
you do every day.
I can just see you in Obedience School.
Duh!

You seem to sense that Roxy
your best friend who died last year,
your fellow running mate,
you two who were inseparable
is buried behind the barn which she is.
We guess you'd like to rest next to Roxy
when your time comes
and because you're a country dog
we could just probably pull it off,
but never in the city
in some busy neighborhood
where they have laws against burying pets,
even if there was room.

You might even end up in a Pet Cemetery
where each dog has a head stone
that gives its name
and when it was born and died
and maybe has a little dog statue on top.

So keeping all things in mind,
I guess its not too bad a deal
being a country dog.
You sleep under the stars,
beg when you're hungry,
eat whatever you please
and not that stuff
that comes out of a bag like wood chips.
You have fun scaring people
with your barking.
You roll around smelly stuff
in the pasture
and clean off in the creek.

When it's all said and done,
there are a couple of songs
that probably tell it like it is for you.
Something about hating fences
and being born free.

The Robin Showbird

A robin skipped across the dewy grass,
paused, cocked his lordly head
with sharpened ears alert to wormy stirrings
like a pointer on a hunt
and luckless, he pranced forward.

How noble
how theatrical that pose
that Barrymore profile
that barrel-chested showbird
who two-stepped across his emerald stage
and found a tiny sanctuary
beneath a frond of zebra grass,
his tiny salon
where a shaft of morning sun
broke through
and brightened up his hideaway.
And in the seclusion of his leafy bower
began his morning toilette.

Down dropped the puffy chest
below his glossy cummerbund
now just a saggy belly.
Prickly feathers under orange
wrinkled up his shirt.
Well safe from peering eyes or predators
he stared into a mirrored water droplet
and rubbed his eyes for morning sand.
Slack beaked, he checked for coated tongue.

One more look at his reflection
and finished with his ritual,
he rested momentarily.
(How great to be offstage)
Then gathering himself
as if commanded to attention
he prepared himself for takeoff.

Out swelled the full-blown chest.
How firm the princely head!
How sleek the silken vest!
How imperious the gaze!
Then one more look for predators
and assuming he was safe,
took one more strut
across the drying grass
and quietly flew away.

Ordering Information

To order copies of
"Growing Up In My Little Italy"
please contact:

Dominick Tammetta
615 Laurel Lake Rd.
Deposit, NY 13754

Email: Dlaurellake@aol.com

Book cost: $9.95, plus $.75 sales tax,
$2.50 shipping and handling, totalling $13.25.

Write Your Memories Here